Once in a while a study comes along, changing how you look at things so completely, you wonder "How did I not see that before?"...this is one such study. Jennifer does a great job taking it one step at a time, fleshing things out, making it very relatable. Using God's Word she shines a bright light on the human condition—on things we all deal with—teaching us to recognize these issues while learning to apply Gods truth to each one, resulting in a new approach to walking in victory. I can't tell you what my favorite part was about this study, because I loved it all—but I can tell you it will continue to bless you long after it's completed. ~Maggie Summers

WHITE

Replacing our Issues
with the
Covering of Christ

JENNIFER WADDLE

All scripture quotations, unless otherwise indicated, are taken from the Holy Bible, New International Version®, NIV®. Copyright ©1973, 1978, 1984, 2010 by Biblica, Inc.™ Used by permission of Zondervan. All rights reserved worldwide. www.zondervan.com

Scripture taken from the New King James Version®. Copyright © 1982 by Thomas Nelson. Used by permission. All rights reserved.

∼ Contents ∼

∼ Introduction ∼

I'm tired, aren't you? I am weary of the issues that weigh me down. We all have them, you know. And though we struggle with similar things, our issues are as individual to us as the color of our eyes. But we all have one very important thing in common. We were created to be clothed with Christ. May I say that again? *We were created to be clothed with Christ.*

The issues we deal with, such as insecurity, anger or pride, can be worn so long, we forget they are not a part of who we were made to be. We often think, *it is just how I am and I will never change.*

But the prophet Isaiah says, **"…He has clothed me with garments of salvation and arrayed me in a robe of righteousness."(Isaiah 61:10)** This reminds us that the things we *choose* to wear in this life are often not from the Lord.

In Scarves of White, we will be coming face to face with the garments that bind us. We will be opening the "drawers of our issues," and giving them a good cleaning out. Why? Because it is time to *"throw off everything that hinders, and the sin that so easily entangles, and run with perseverance the race marked out for us." (Hebrews 12:1)*

I'm tired, aren't you? Tired of letting my issues get in the way of truly living for God. But I know just the solution. *"The Word of God is living and active. Sharper than any double-edged sword, it penetrates even to dividing the soul and spirit, joints and marrow; it judges the thoughts and attitudes of the heart. Nothing in all creation is hidden from God's sight. Everything is uncovered and laid bare before the eyes of Him to Whom we must give account." (Hebrews 4:12-13)*

Ladies, as we dig deep to get to the root of what confines us, and what may even render us ineffective for Christ, we will be reminded that His power is made perfect in our weaknesses. There is nothing to fear; for the God of the universe has given us everything we need for life and godliness through Him!

My prayer for you, (and for me), is that whatever things we are dealing with, whatever 'scarves' don't belong, will be replaced with the most beautiful garment of all…the covering of Christ.

Your Fellow Scarf Wearer,

Jennifer

How to Use this Study:

Scarves of White is a seven-week study intended for a personal or small group setting. Each Session is followed by three days of journal-based homework. You can expect to spend around twenty minutes on each assignment; very manageable for busy girls!

With the exception of Session One, each Session is preceded by Discussion Questions of the previous week's homework.

In a group setting, The Bible Study Leader can read the Sessions aloud, followed by discussion, prayer and fellowship.

Another option would be for each participant to read through the Session at home and come prepared to share their insights, with leader guidance. All leaders and co-leaders of this study should preview each Session and look up the Scriptures ahead of time. This will insure the best use of time and help keep things on schedule. If Scarves of White is a personal study, then simply go through the book chronologically.

Finally, it is very important to leave adequate time for prayer. I have found that during this study, prayer requests are abundant, and we need to take those requests very seriously and not rush through them.

A notebook or journal can be used instead of the journal pages provided.

"In the beginning You laid the foundations of the earth, and the heavens are the work of Your hands. They will perish but You remain; they will all wear out like a garment. Like clothing You will change them and they will be discarded. But You remain the same and Your years will never end." (Psalm 102:25-27)

∽One ∽

Got Issues?

I have to admit, I'm not much of a scarf wearer. I've always felt like my shoulders are too broad, and my neck too thick for a scarf. But I like them. I think they look great on others. And the choices of colors and styles are endless!

I do, however, wear *emotional or habitual* scarves every day. And some of them aren't flattering.

Now, I have to tell you, that when I first came up with the idea for this Bible study, I was originally going to call it The Unmentionables of Womanhood. You know, our unmentionables, as in *underwear*. But I just couldn't envision pulling different colored underwear out of the drawer as examples of our issues. Don't you agree? ☺

Over the next few weeks, we will be taking a hard look at some of the most common things women face. These issues supersede age, status and personality. They are habits, attitudes, beliefs and strongholds that women of all walks of life face.

Although there are probably a hundred different issues, I narrowed it down to the ones I have either seen most often, or dealt with myself. And I've assigned each a color.

Red: Anger

Blue: Discontentment

Yellow: Insecurity

Purple: Pride

Black: Oppression

If you are apprehensive or unsure whether this study is for you, hang in there. Just showing up to see what it is about, is a good indication that you are dealing with some unwanted issues. Once we dive into the Word of God, I have no doubt He will speak to your heart and give you the confirmation you need. Speaking of God's Word…

*Please open your Bibles to Isaiah chapter 1

We will be taking a look at a few verses from this Old Testament chapter, but before we do, let's refresh our minds a bit with who Isaiah was and who his listening audience was.

Isaiah lived during the time that the Kingdom of Israel was divided. The Assyrians had come in and taken 10 of the 12 tribes captive in 722 BC. Those ten tribes became the Northern Kingdom, or *Israel,* and the two remaining tribes became known as the Southern Kingdom, or *Judah.* Confused yet? I sure hope not.

You see, Isaiah was sent by God to warn Israel and Judah, and to condemn their backsliding ways. But he also spoke of repentance and salvation to anyone who would turn back to God.

*Let's read Isaiah 1:1-3

"Hear, O heavens! Listen, O earth! For the Lord has spoken; "I reared up children and brought them up, but they have rebelled against Me. The ox knows his master, the donkey his owner's manager, but Israel does not know, My people do not understand."

As Christians, we too have been brought up by the Lord. We are His children. Through His Word, His Spirit and His purpose we have been raised with Christ. But in our issues we are like the Israelites. We have forgotten our Maker. We have misunderstood His divine purpose for us and have allowed things like discontentment, pride and insecurity lead us astray.

Now, it sounds much nicer to say we have an *issue* with insecurity rather than a *sin* of insecurity. Believe me, I don't like to think of my issues as sin either. I would rather be a victim of my issues than to admit I may be walking in rebellion.

But Ladies, we have fallen prey to these things far too long. I've seen strongholds hinder people's walk with the Lord, and I've experienced it myself. We are all battling them, and because you are here, it seems you've made the decision to deal with them.

*Take a look at Isaiah 1:16-17

"...wash and make yourselves clean...stop doing wrong, learn to do right! Seek justice, encourage the oppressed. Defend the cause of the fatherless, plead the case of the widow."

I love the action words Isaiah uses here. Wash, Make, Stop, Learn, Seek, Encourage, Defend and Plead... these words are motivating! But I have experienced time and time again, being too bound by my issues to even consider encouraging or defending anyone.

Now, to my favorite verse from Isaiah 1... verse 18.

"Come now, let us reason together," says the Lord. "Though your sins are like scarlet, they shall be white as snow; though they are crimson, they shall be like wool."

Familiar? I hope so.

I love how the Lord says, *"...let us reason together..."* That gives me such hope! We are not facing these challenges alone. Let's keep that in mind as we take a close look at each scarf over the next few weeks. We will need Him every step of the way.

It is amazing to me that Isaiah received a vision of what Jesus would do on the cross. More than seven hundred years before Christ was born, Isaiah got a glimpse of the Messiah.

Our scarlet sins became whiter than snow the minute we first believed. Our crimson-stained selves were washed white like wool. And that garment, the garment of salvation, remains. But each day we decide that a little color won't hurt. A little pride...a little anger... a bit of insecurity...and soon our true color is covered up.

Some of us are still asking the question...*Why would I want to confront my issues when it would be much easier to accept them as just a part of who I am?*

<u>Because Ladies, they were never intended to be a part of who we were created to be.</u>

I'd like for us to take a look at several Scripture passages that affirm who we really are in the Lord. And if there are any doubts remaining as to whether or not you can overcome your issues, these verses will encourage you.

*Let's read Genesis 1:27, Psalm 139:13-16, Ephesians 2:10, 4: 17-24, and Revelation 4:11

These verses confirm why our issues are not a part of who we really are.

1. We were created in the image of God.
2. We were fearfully and wonderfully made, and all of our days were ordained by God.
3. He has called us by name; He is with us; He is our God, and we are precious to Him.
4. We were created for His glory!
5. We are God's workmanship, created in Christ Jesus to do good works, prepared in advance for us.
6. We must no longer live in the futility of our thinking.
7. We must put off our old self.
8. We must be made new in the attitude of our minds.
9. We must put on our new self, created to be like God in true righteousness and holiness.
10. And finally, He is worthy to receive glory, honor and power, for we were created by His will.

This week, we may be surprised at what the Lord reveals as we open our drawers and see the shades of yellow or red, blue or purple. But remember, the Scarf of White, pure and holy, resembling the covering of Christ, is always there. We may cover it up, but it remains.

This Bible study may be a little different than what you are used to. It isn't the typical question and answer type of study. It is journal-based, and I encourage you to write down meaningful answers as the Lord leads you, even if you aren't much of a writer. By writing things down, we are able to see in black and white what we are facing. And the good thing is, years later, you will be able to go back and read where you *once were* and how far the Lord has brought you.

I realize some of you are not into journaling, and I respect that. My husband would rather chop his hand off than journal! But this is for your benefit. It's designed to lead you deeper into the Bible, further your prayer life, and take you a little out of your comfort zone.

Your journal pages will be for *your eyes only.* You will have an opportunity to share, but only if you want to. There is no pressure from me to finish your homework. However, I have assigned only three lessons each week. I know how busy you are, and I feel like three days of homework is very attainable. You can expect to spend about twenty minutes on the assignments, so I hope you will complete all of them. They will be very crucial to this study.

Please remember that we are in this together, and more importantly, God is reasoning it out with us. He longs for us to discard these scarves that don't belong so that His covering of pure white can shine through.

I am praying for each of you and I am grateful to be on this journey with you.

Jennifer Waddle

Am I willing to change?

Let's start out with a little "willingness" quiz.
  1. **I have no issues.**
  2. **Issues are my friend.**
  3. **Ok, I have an issue or two.**
  4. **Help! I am full of issues!**

Which statement describes you best? If I'm completely honest, I have made all of those statements at different times in my life. Prideful, self-confident me may have said, "I have no issues, thank you very much." Complacent, comfortable me probably said, "Issues are my friend." But the *real* me says, I definitely have an issue or two, and on occasion I am full of them!

To be *real* can be very scary. It forces us to be vulnerable and possibly allow others to see our true colors. But ladies, do not let the enemy steal your desire to make some necessary changes. Do not let him kill your determination to take each issue and bring it under the authority of God's Word. And please do not let him distract you from being *who you are in Christ*. God has too many wonderful plans for you!

Before we go any further, let's pray…

"Holy God, Maker of heaven and earth, we come to You today. We want to thank You for making us fearfully and wonderfully. O Lord, how we forget that You are the Potter and we are the clay. You have made us for Your divine purpose and glory. Forgive us Lord, for taking matters into our own hands and going our own way. We want to be conformed to Your likeness day by day. Hear us Father, and heal us. We need You. In Jesus' Name, amen."

The Women's Ministry at my church is called *Hadesh,* which means to *renew or restore.* Psalm 51 is one of the most beautiful passages that David wrote as a heart-felt cry for mercy, forgiveness and the cleansing power of God.

*Please read Psalm 51

These words speak of cleansing, purging, renewing and restoring. Sisters, God can do this for us. He really can!

As we open our drawer of issues we may feel overwhelmed at the sight, or we may think it's no big deal. But *anything* that covers our true identity in Christ needs to go. And the best place to start is by *asking.* King David asked the Lord to deliver him. Look at his words in Psalm 51…

Have mercy…

Blot out…

Wash away…

Cleanse me…

Wash me…

Create in me…

Renew…

Restore…

After David asked the Lord for deliverance, he finished the Psalm with what he would *be free* to do once he was cleansed and renewed. Take a look at verses 13-15.

"Then I will teach transgressors Your ways..."

"My tongue will sing of Your righteousness..."

"My mouth will declare Your praise..."

Ladies, whether we believe it or not, our issues hold us back from fully living for God, and we need the cleansing power of the Holy Spirit! Will you ask the Lord for a renewed heart today? Will you use the words of David as a spring-board to pen your own requests?

Take a few minutes to write down a prayer of renewal. Use the eight phrases David used to help guide you, starting with "Have mercy..."

Remember, I am on this journey with you. I'll see you back here for Day Two.

Journal...

_____

_____

_____

_____

_____

"Sorry Brudder"

Our assignment yesterday was to form a prayer from Psalm 51, asking God to renew and deliver us from the issues that have taken hold. It may have been a challenge to admit our sin before God, as David did.

Does it seem offensive to call our issues sin? I sure hope not. There is certainly no condemnation here. I, too, would rather believe the issues in my life are merely minor irritations that don't really matter. But they do.

As of today, my grandsons are two years old, and eight months old. Noah is the big brother, and James is the baby. And oh what lessons of faith I learn as I observe them! As a Nana, I am soooo much more relaxed than I was when my kids were little. Things that would normally frustrate me now make me turn my head to hide my laughter.

Recently, I had the boys over and Noah was getting a little wild around the baby. Sure enough, he ended up accidentally pushing him over. Little James took it well, but trying to be a good Nana, I said, "Noah, be careful. Now what do you say to James?"

Not sure how he would respond, I was surprised to see him bend down, eye-to eye, pat his head and say, "Sorry Brudder." It was the cutest thing!

Today we will be looking at what it means to be truly sorry. We will see that there is a difference between godly sorrow and earthly sorrow.

*Please read 2 Corinthians 7:10-11

This passage expresses Paul's love and concern for the Christians in Corinth. He was encouraging them, by letter, to repent and let godly sorrow produce a desire to see justice done. He wasn't trying to hurt them, but *help* them.

One of my deepest prayers in this study is that I will be able to help you discard the unwanted scarves. It pains me to see women bound by their issues, unable to live freely for Jesus. And because I battle my own issues, *only by the grace of God* am I able to help others.

In my mid-twenties I had an addiction to cigarettes. They were a source of comfort to me and a way to relieve stress. However, I didn't want my house to smell like smoke so I got in the habit of rising early before my family was awake, and taking my cup of coffee out on the porch. There, I would pray and marvel at the beauty of God's creation, sip my coffee…and smoke.

One morning I was doing that very thing when I suddenly found it very difficult to pray. I thought it might be that I was distracted by the morning sounds of traffic and birds, etc., but as I sat there puffing away, I felt deeply for the first time that my sinful habit had wedged its way between me and the Lord. And you know what? I was filled with *godly sorrow*. I threw the cigarettes away and never looked back.

Paul pointed out what *godly sorrow* would produce in the Corinthians. Look at his words.

Earnestness

Eagerness

Indignation

Alarm

Longing

Concern

Readiness

You see, that morning on my porch, I was **alarmed** that it was difficult to pray. I had a **longing** to reconnect with God. I was very **concerned** that my sin had come between us. And I was **ready** to give up cigarettes forever.

Sisters, how I want that for all of us in every area! I pray that every time we choose that scarf of pride or anger, insecurity or discontentment, it will be so uncomfortable we won't be able to wear it.

Our repentance must go far deeper than a shallow "I'm sorry." And I believe it begins with a 'want to.'

Years ago, I took a study where the Leader prayed that God would change her 'want to.' Can we pray that today? *"Lord, please change my 'want to.'"*

Please read 2Corinthians 7:10-11 again. Read it slowly. Pause to pray and let God speak to you.

Dear Ones, is there an **earnestness** in your step? An **eagerness** in your mind? **Indignation** to stay the course? **Alarm** bells alerting you? A **longing** to be free from the scarves that entangle?

Today's assignment is simple. Ponder the words of our passage, and answer the questions above as honestly as you can.

I pray for great peace to wash over you as you complete this assignment. I'll see you back for Day Three.

Journal...

_____

_____

_____

_____

_____

_____

_____

_____

_____

_____

_____

_____

_____

_____

_____

_____

Decisions…Decisions…

As we wind down our first week of study, I want to leave you with a detailed passage in Colossians. It is a passage of decision.

*Please read Colossians 3: 1-17

As we read these verses, Paul reminds us that we have taken off our old selves and put on our new selves, and that we are renewed in the image of our Creator. Now, how do we know he is speaking to us and not only the believers of that day? The first verse is our answer.

"Since then, you have been raised with Christ, set your hearts on things above, where Christ is seated at the right hand of God."

Sisters, we have indeed been raised with Christ! From the moment we first believed and put our trust in Him, we were saved from hell and raised with Him to everlasting life. It is imperative to set our hearts and minds on things above!

How often is your mind set on things above?

In verse five, Paul does not mince words when he says, *"Put to death, therefore, whatever belongs to your earthly nature."*

The phrase, "put to death," in Greek, means to: *destroy the strength of, deprive of power…*

My husband works at the City Power Plant where coal is used to generate power for Colorado Springs. You wouldn't believe the work that goes into generating power!

One of the jobs there is to make sure the boiler runs smoothly. Without proper balance of air- flow, good coal, and numerous other factors, objects called 'clinkers' will build up in the boiler. These clinkers are made up of molten ash and can get as big as a car!

Sometimes, when the clinkers get big enough, they have to shut the unit off, which means they deprive it of power. In some cases, they have a team of people who come in and use explosives to break the giant clinkers apart. Talk about destroying the strength of something!

Sisters, when it comes to our issues, we need to make the decision to deprive them of their strength over us, and destroy any power they hold.

Will you **decide** today to deal with the issues that hold you back?

We are getting ready to face these scarves one-by-one, and I hope this week has prepared you to confront them with the Word of God.

Some of us may feel like we are carrying burdens the size of big old clinkers, but there is a team of One who will come and blow them to bits. *Father, Son and Holy Spirit…*

Ladies, God wants us to be exactly who He created us to be, nothing more…nothing less. He wants to uncover the beautiful Scarf of White He set upon us when He clothed us with His Son. The question is, will we let Him?

As we end our first week of homework, I would like you to write a statement of decision. It can be as long or short as you want. You can write it as a prayer, as a commitment, or as a goal, but ultimately it is a **decision** to do away with the things that entangle you.

Are you ready to make a decision? I am. In fact, I am going to write my statement of decision right here. I am not proud of my issues, and I would rather ignore them sometimes. But I want to change. And I want the accountability that comes from walking this journey with all of you.

Statement of Decision:

July 3, 2014

I decide today to face my issues head-on. They are not a part of who I was created to be. Forgive me Lord for choosing to wear things that are not of You. I want to be free of them. I want my life to bring You glory. I don't want to be held back by sinful habits, thoughts or attitudes any longer. Please deal with my issues in such a way that they will be deprived of power, for it is only by Your Spirit that I can live totally for You. Thank You Lord for your unfailing love and faithfulness. I trust You to be my help in time of need. In Jesus' Name I commit this to You...

Jennifer

Journal...

_____

_____

_____

_____

_____

_____

_____

_____

∼ Homework Discussion Questions ∼

Week One: *Got Issues?*

(To be shared at the beginning of Week Two)

1. You were challenged to use Psalm 51 as a personal prayer of renewal. Was that difficult for you?
2. How do you feel about calling your issues "sin"?
3. As we learned what it meant to have godly sorrow, how did that affect the way you look at your issues?
4. An example was given as a word picture of *depriving our issues of power*. What are some practical ways we can do that?
5. Any other thoughts about our willingness to deal with our issues?

Looking Ahead

"...for man's anger does not bring about the righteous life that God desires." (James 1:20)

~Two~
Scarf of Red...*Anger*

'She's Mean...She's Mad'

Of all the issues we will cover in this Bible Study, anger has been one of the biggest for me. Not only did I *learn* anger, I *adopted* it as my way of life. Irritated at the slightest thing, wanting to be heard, getting especially upset if anything tainted my image, anger used to be a regular part of my existence.

When my oldest son David was three or four years old, I got a huge wake-up call. Having filled my schedule with various activities, I was often in a hurry and not in the best of moods.

One morning, I was gathering our things together and the boys were playing on the front porch. I had the door open and could hear them. Pretty soon I heard David say, "She's mean. She's mad. She's mean. She's mad."

Peeking around the corner, I saw him holding two action figures, having them say to each other, "She's mean. She's mad. My mom is mean and mad." He was talking about me!

Shame, guilt and deep sorrow filled my heart that day. I realized anger was something that I had allowed as my way of life. I was one grumpy mama! The thing is, it had nothing to do with the children, but everything to do with my perspective and priorities. I had resorted to yelling at the drop of a hat, and giving looks that could kill. But that day, it clicked. I made a decision to say, "No more." No more letting anger get the best of me.

Now, maybe you don't have a problem with persistent anger. Praise God! But I'll bet you have someone in your life that does. And it is not fun.

To watch someone let their anger get the best of them is like watching a pressure cooker build up steam, ready to blow. Everyone around them gets tense. And you know what? It's unnecessary. It really is.

Once I recognized my tendency toward anger and made the decision to uproot it, things got a lot better in my relationships.

Now, I'm not talking about the occasional frustration that happens to all of us. I am speaking about the sinful anger that consistently rules thoughts, words and actions. If you struggle with it at all, you know what I am talking about.

The very first example of anger in the Bible goes back to Cain. Firstborn son of Adam and Eve, and brother of Abel, you know the story. But I love the words that the Lord spoke directly to Cain…a warning that sin was right at his door.

*Let's read Genesis 4:1-8

This account always makes me want to shout, "Don't do it Cain! See that sin crouching in the doorway? Get a broom and sweep it away! Hurry!"

But verse 8 tells us exactly how Cain responded. It was as if he didn't even hear the words of the Lord.

We can be like that too. The Holy Spirit, mighty in power, so mighty He raised Jesus from the dead, speaks to us…warns us…says, "Sin is crouching at your door!" And what do we do? Proceed as if we do not hear Him.

Anger is like that. This red scarf is so bold and brazen it flashes like lightening and starts a spark that quickly becomes a flame and eventually a raging fire.

*Let's read James 1: 19-21, and 3: 7-10

Quick to listen, slow to speak, and slow to become angry is the advice given by James. Yet, a persistently angry person usually doesn't listen very well, *or* remain silent. In verse 21, James states we should get rid of the evil and humbly accept the Word planted in us. Hmmm…humbly accept.

Unrighteous anger has the shortest fuse, and the quickest explosion. Even when we try to suppress it, our thoughts can become outright murderous if we aren't careful.

*Please read Matthew 5:21-22

The New King James Version says, ***"Whoever is angry with his brother without a cause shall be in danger of the judgment."*** That word *cause* in Greek means: *vainly or to no purpose*. And that's what sinful anger does. It has no good reason, and no valid purpose. You're just 'mean and mad.'

Is there a type of anger that is good? Yes.

*Take a look at the perfect example in John 2:13-17

Jesus' actions and words were a clear example of someone who was angry, but did not sin. He made a whip, he over-turned tables, and he commanded the money changers to leave. Some might say he was out of control. But no…

It was zeal for God's house that consumed Him and ultimately motivated Him to do what He did. He had a purpose…a Divine purpose.
If your child ran into the street, would you slowly go get him and gently lead him back to safety, all the while smiling and patting him on the back? No! In our great love for our kids, and zeal for their safety, we would run to get them, shout "Danger!" and hopefully frighten them enough that they would never do it again.

This is where it gets tricky. You see, we like to *justify* our anger and tell ourselves we have a right to react the way we do. But how do we test it to make sure it is righteous anger?

*Look at Ephesians 4:26-27, 29-32

"In your anger do not sin."
Ok, we gather from this that we will get angry. It's a part of life. Many things in this world are going to make us mad. But we are to deal with

it properly and promptly. The longer we let it linger and fester, the more likely it is the devil will gain a foothold.

"Let no corrupt word proceed out of your mouth."

Now we know that when we witness someone's wrath, we hear all sorts of awful things. Especially when we are full of tension, just like the steaming pot on the stove, we'd better think before we speak. Take a moment to pray and ask…how can I say this with integrity and grace? How can I speak the truth firmly, but with kindness and love?

Fortunately I was there that day, to hear Batman telling Spider Man that I was 'mean and mad.' It woke me up. It made me realize my quick-to-anger issue had to be dealt with.

Now, since that day, I have yelled. I have gotten grumpy, and I have sinned in my anger. But I have to say it is no longer the norm. It is rare. And it is because I made a *decision* to stop sinful anger in its tracks.

This week, we will be looking at why anger becomes a stronghold. Whether it be a learned behavior, a protective front, or even manipulation at getting what we want, we are gonna face it. But don't worry. We will also get into the Word and learn the "how to." With God's divine help, anger can crouch at our door all day long, but we will not give in to it.

I'm excited about what the Lord will do in each of us this week. Please do the devotions. We need the Word of God like we need bread and water.

✝ Week Two Homework/Day One

Angry at God?

The words, *slow to anger and abounding in love*, are mentioned several times across the Old and New Testaments, and they describe our God perfectly.

Joel 2:13 says that the Lord is *"...slow to anger and of great kindness."*

Remember the example of Cain during our session together?

Something was mentioned in that passage that pointed to one source of Cain's anger. *"His offering to God was not accepted, but Abel's was."* **(Genesis 4:3-5)**

Now, in the psychological phenomena of our day, we would analyze this to death. We would surmise that if Cain had felt accepted and favored he wouldn't have become angry enough to murder his brother. But remember God's words. *"If you do what is right, will you not be accepted?"* **(Genesis 4:7)**

Cain must have felt it would be easier to murder his brother than simply do what was right. His anger toward Abel and toward God overcame any desire to do the right thing.

Do we let anger overcome us like that, to the point where we no longer desire to do the right thing, but the angry thing? Someone else in the Bible had an anger issue…

Jonah, our seafaring friend, didn't want to do what the Lord asked of him and nearly got a whole crew of people killed. Coming close to death himself, he finally went to Nineveh, and the Ninevites repented. But Jonah got mad. Really mad.

*Please read Jonah 3:10-4:11

His own displeasure was at the root of his anger. God's mercy on Nineveh didn't please him. Basically, things weren't working out the way Jonah thought they should. He thought those sinful, ruthless people deserved judgment not mercy.

Ladies, the Bible says there was revival in the heart of the king! He commanded the people to turn from their evil ways, and they did. Why would this make Jonah angry? If there was to be a great revival in America, wouldn't we all rejoice?

But think for a minute. What if there was repentance in the hearts of people who had done us the most harm? If one of today's terrorist groups, that had caused us much suffering, turned from evil and sought the One true God, it would be a good thing, right?

Yes, a very good thing.

But our human nature, like Jonah's, might resent the fact that they "got away" with so much evil and were now being spared by God. We might want revenge.

Jonah even went so far as to find a place outside the city to watch and see if God would destroy it. Selfish anger does that, my friends. It does not rejoice when it should rejoice. It cannot accept God's divine favor when it should accept it. And it all has to do with *self.*

Jonah was selfishly angry with God. *He* wanted to see Nineveh destroyed. *He* wanted the comfort of the vine shading him from the hot sun. But when he didn't get his way, he was angry enough to die.

Sisters, is it possible you are angry at God for your present circumstances? Are you disappointed in life and blame Him?

These are tough questions, I know. But I want you to spend some time in prayer today searching your heart.

You may have struggled with sinful anger so long you don't even know what the root of it is. But if there is any chance it is directed toward the Lord, admit it and repent of it. He knows your heart already!

*For your journaling assignment, I'd like you to be creative. Now some of you are going to want to skip this, but please give it your best effort. On the left side of the page write the letters of the word "ANGER" vertically. Now, as an acrostic, write words or phrases for each letter. Here is an example:

Always hurts

Not beneficial

Grows into resentment

Excludes people

Rages like a fire

Ladies, I want the sinful effects of anger to be clear so that we won't fall into its trap again. Thank you for spending time on this exercise. I will see you back here for Day Two.

Journal…

Red in the Face

The color red is displayed at Christmas, Valentine's Day, and Birthdays. Poppies and Geraniums are vibrant and beautiful. Apples, strawberries and cherries were colored by God, our Wonderful Creator.

But red is also a color we think of when someone is very angry. The heated flush that comes over a person when their anger is at the boiling point, is a real, physiological event.

Studies have shown that some people actually *see* the color red when they are angry. Medical Science can detect changes in the brain, like the increase of adrenaline. The frontal lobe contains our reasoning center, and when the emotion of anger is triggered, the amygdala (uh-mig-duh-luh) begins working over-time! Blood rushes to the frontal lobe in an attempt to calm things down. That is one good reason for counting to ten before we react. It gives our brains time to defuse our anger. Interesting, huh?

When I think of someone red-in-the-face, I'm reminded of the cartoon character Elmer Fudd trying to catch Bugs Bunny, "that Wascally Wabbit," and getting so mad steam would come out of his ears.

But Ladies, aside from the outward effects of anger, the effects of the heart are far more serious.

Let's get into the Word. Please find a quiet place and really ask God for wisdom. We sure need it!

*Please read: Proverbs 22:24-25, 29:11, 22 & James 1:19-21

We see several things about anger in these verses.

1. We can be ensnared by someone else's anger.
2. We should avoid being around a hot-tempered person.
3. It is *wise* to keep our anger under control.
4. Anger causes dissension and many sins.
5. Anger does not bring about the righteous life God desires.

Pretty basic, right? We know these things. But when the red scarf has been a part of us so long, we tend to justify it.

And what is the biggest warning sign that anger is about to get the best of us?

The Holy Spirit…

When we feel that first wave of frustration, and there is the *stirring of the Spirit* in our souls, we had better listen. Just as God warned Cain, He warns us as well.

*Today's assignment is to really think about what makes you angry. From big to small, write it all down. Is there constant frustration in your life? Is there bitterness or resentment brewing? Are you quick to yell? Stomp around and throw things? Stew quietly? Think murderous thoughts?

As you write, commit all of it to God and ask for His help and His mercy. Great is His faithfulness! Remember, your journaling is for your eyes only. You won't be made to share anything with the group. The main thing is that you are sharing it with God and letting His loving-kindness wash over you.

See you back here for Day Three.

Journal…

_____
_____
_____
_____
_____
_____
_____
_____
_____
_____
_____
_____
_____
_____
_____
_____
_____
_____
_____
_____
_____
_____

✝ Week Two Homework/ Day Three

Love Wash over Us

As you know, this is our last day of homework for Week Two. Remember, I have kept the homework minimal so that you will not feel overwhelmed. But please remain in the Word *every day,* and continue to pray fervently for others on this journey.

Yesterday we wrote down a list of things that make us angry. I hope you were able to complete that exercise. And I pray you were able to be completely honest.

*Today, we are going to look at that list again, but this time we are going to write *truths* across from those anger issues. For example:

My Anger Issue	God's Truth
I get angry when I don't get my way…	My ways are not His ways, nor my thoughts His thoughts. The Bible says to yield to one another in Christ Jesus.

Really spend time in the Word finding just the right verses to counter the things that make you mad.

As we wrap up the issue of anger and 'oust' this red scarf once and for all, I want to encourage you with some heartfelt words…

Sister, whatever has caused this turmoil within you, whatever has prompted this deep-seeded frustration with everyone and everything, anger is no way to handle it. Stop. Stop and look around. Take a deep breath and let the peace of God wash over you. Don't you long for His peace? Let the scarf of red fall away as you pull the gorgeous, white scarf of Jesus a little tighter…

My favorite Christian artist, Sara Groves, wrote a song called "When it was over." The chorus is simple. It says, *"Love wash over a multitude of things… Love wash over a multitude of things… Make us whole…"*

This song kept coming to mind as I was searching for a solution to our issue of anger. And isn't love the ultimate remedy? Not our shallow, human love that shifts like the changing weather, but God's great love…

If Cain would have truly loved his brother…

If Jonah could have loved the Ninevites…

If I would have loved my boys too much to be mean and mad all the time…

Love wash over a multitude of things…

In closing this week, let's look at one more passage.

*Please read Ephesians 4:29-32

Is it truthful to say that it grieves the Holy Spirit when we let bitterness, wrath, anger, clamor, and evil speaking come out of us?

If there be any reason at all to finally discard the red scarf, let it be so that *we will not grieve the Holy Spirit.*

Love wash over us… as anger comes. Love wash over us… as we stop to pray. Love wash over us… as we yield to one another in brotherly love. Love wash over a multitude of things.
Let's Pray…

"Gracious God, abounding in love, we come before You humbly today. We are so weary of the anger that flares up at the least little thing. We lay it down. We want Your peace more than anything. We want to love our brothers and sisters so much that we will not let our anger get the best of us anymore. Lord, we hear You when You warn us that sin is right at our doorstep. And we ask in the name of Jesus that You sweep it away. Thank You, Father, for releasing us from the stronghold of anger. We love You. In Jesus Name, amen."

Have a great week and I will see you for Week Three.

Jennifer Waddle

∽ Homework Discussion Questions ∽

Week Two: Anger

(To be shared at the beginning of Week Three)

1. We looked at the lives of Cain and Jonah and their examples of anger at God. How easy is it for you to blame God for circumstances in your life?
2. Jesus displayed righteous anger when driving the money-changers out of the temple. What are other examples of righteous anger? If you are willing, share what things make you really angry.
3. We were challenged to let God's truths wash over our issues of anger. Would anyone like to share the truths they found?
4. Any other thoughts on the issue of anger?

Looking Ahead

"...I have learned the secret of being content in any and every situation, whether well fed or hungry, whether living in plenty or in want. I can do everything through Him who gives me strength." Philippians 4:12

Jennifer Waddle

∼Three ∼
Scarf of Blue...*Discontentment*

"Don't it Make My Brown Eyes Blue"

When I was a kid my parents were steeped in the 70s, along with disco lessons, bell-bottoms and even afros. One of the many songs they played on our record player or eight-track was the song, "Don't It Make My Brown Eyes Blue," by Crystal Gayle. The reason I remember the song so well is because Crystal Gayle had long, long, hair, almost to her ankles. Oh how I wanted hair like that! And when I think of the issue of discontentment, I think of that song.

Discontentment touches each of us at one time or another. We get restless, bored, and weary of the day-to-day. But when does discontentment become sin in our lives?

It becomes sin when *we are never satisfied with what we've been given, and when we find it difficult to thank God for His abundant blessings.* Ladies, discontentment can grow into a very ominous and dark cloud that not only makes us miserable, but also those around us.

Only a few years ago I found myself so discontent I didn't know what I wanted. I remember thinking, "Is this all there is to life?" And unfortunately it brought a lot of stress to my husband who was a wonderful provider. I wanted to move to another house, another state, another country. I wanted him to change jobs from a job he loved. I wanted to adopt. I wanted more vacations. I wanted...wanted...wanted.

But something very profound happened the summer my father-in-law was diagnosed with pancreatic cancer. Given only months to live, he took the whole Waddle clan on a trip to Cancun Mexico. There were thirteen of us and we had a special, yet bittersweet time together.

One evening, as everyone was playing with a giant chess set near one of the resort pools, I snuck away a few yards to the beach. The moon was shining bright over the water, and the waves were coming in. Stars were everywhere and I felt so small standing alone on that beach. As I found the Big Dipper, and then the Little Dipper, my eyes were drawn to a star formation I had never seen. It was the perfect formation of a cross. I thought maybe my eyes were playing tricks on me.

But as I gazed at that cross in the sky, it was as if God was saying, *"I have given you everything, yet you appreciate nothing."*

I was cut to the heart and wept at my discontentment. I repented of my sinful ungratefulness, and from that moment on I was changed. In fact, I was ready to go home that night! I didn't need Cancun. I didn't need a new house. I didn't need a thing.

Persistent discontentment with what we have or who we are is like a slap in the face to God. It is like saying, "The cross is not enough."

We begin to see things in such a dim light that we are convinced we are deprived of something we deserve. And that is when we take matters into our own hands. We either choose to be a martyr of sorts, walking around with a frown, shoulders slumped, and with a persistent feeling of defeat. Or, we make rash decisions that can be as destructive as a tornado sweeping through town. Both ways of handling discontentment are actions saying, "God has not fulfilled my desires, therefore I will take my desires into my own hands."

Ladies, stop for a minute to think of a typical day. We wake up on a bed, under soft covers. We push a button for coffee. We open our cupboards full of food.

Do we realize there is a vast percentage of women on this earth who do not have such luxuries? They do not wake up thinking they might go and get a hair-cut that day, or buy a new rug for the entryway. They do not get to decide what they will make for dinner.

Now I'm not trying to sound like a mother who says, "Clean your plate. There are people in Africa who don't get to eat."

But I am trying to put our spirit of discontentment in perspective. We are some of the most blessed people. We have an abundance that we don't even recognize. And yet we wake up depressed, dissatisfied, unhappy...

I've seen discontentment ruin marriages. I have seen it embitter people. I've seen it cause major debt. I've seen it change people into pleasure seeking individuals where nothing is ever enough. And I have miserably lived it out myself.

Let's look at the classic, Biblical example of discontentment.

*Please read Numbers 11:1-2, 4-6, &18-20

Now to the Israelite's defense, I'm sure it was no picnic in the desert. They were unsettled and uncertain of the future. In their humanness, they had physical cravings for food other than manna. And when they would go a couple of days without water they were thirsty.

But God knew what they needed. Matthew 6:32 states that God *knows* we need food and drink and clothing. The Israelite's complaints had grown far beyond a request for food and water.

*Look at Numbers 14:2-4

"Wouldn't it be better for us to go back to Egypt?"

Listen to the severity of that question! The Israelites had forgotten the mighty hand of God and His deliverance. They began to long for a place that had been ruthless and oppressive to them.

You see, if we let discontentment remain long enough, it clouds our vision. It skews our memory. It deceives us into thinking anything is better than what we have. And it robs us of a grateful heart toward God. Sisters, this may be the reason why the scarf of blue invades your life. You may *know* that you ought to be grateful in every circumstance, but when discontentment covers you, it is near impossible to give thanks.

This week we are going to see what it means to be content with what we have and who we were created to be. We already know what discontentment is and what it feels like. We need to know what *contentment* looks and feels like.

Please don't skip the short journaling assignments this week. Hopefully, they will give insight as to why you are battling this issue and how you can conquer it.

⌗ Week Three Homework/Day One

Dream Life...

Have you ever imagined what a perfect life or even a perfect day might look like? I have often said that I would make a good princess. You know, the fairytale kind who rises late and eats crumpets and sips tea? Every wish is at her command...

Then there is reality. The perfect day as a wife, mom, home-schooler, writer, musician, daughter, friend, neighbor etc...frankly doesn't exist. One morning last year, I got up extra early. I was burdened and couldn't sleep. As I sipped my coffee, I decided to write on paper what I thought a perfect day would look like. I filled three pages! It included things like rising while it was still dark, making a big breakfast for everyone, writing letters to all my relatives, and cleaning every inch of the house...But at the end of those three pages, I heard the Lord's still, small voice.

"Daughter, Love Me and love others."

"But!" I began to argue. To no avail. The Lord was right.

"Love Me...and love others."

He reminded me that I could be little Miss Homemaker and try to do everything perfectly, but if I didn't have love, I was nothing. A huge dose of contentment filled my soul that morning, because I knew I loved my Jesus. And I knew I loved my family. And I knew my perfect day was summed up in those five words.

"Love Me and love others."

What would your perfect life look like? If you had it your way, would you desire to live like a princess? Would you change anything at all?

I'd like for us to take a look at a very familiar passage. You have most likely read this before, but I am asking you to read it with an open heart once again. The Proverbs 31 woman has been a model of perfection to Christian women across the ages. But is that what the Proverb is really saying about her? That she was perfect? That she had a perfect life?

*Please read Proverbs 31: 10-31

The action words that describe this woman make it seem like she was Superwoman. As you already know, I like to list the major ideas from our Scripture passages. And boy are there a lot of things to list from our Proverbs 31 woman. Take a look...

She brings good not harm...
She selects wool and flax...
She works with eager hands...
She brings her food from afar...
She gets up while it is dark...
She provides food for her family...
She considers a field and buys it...

She plants a vineyard...
She works vigorously...
She sees that her trading is profitable...
She opens her arms to the poor...
She makes bed coverings and linen garments...
She sells them to merchants...
She laughs at the days to come...
She speaks wisdom...
She watches over the affairs of her household...
She fears the Lord...

Does a woman get any more perfect than this? And yet, I do not believe she portrays a life of perfection.

I see a life of *deep contentment*...a woman living within her God-given roles and boundaries.

Remember that old phrase... "Grow where you are planted."?

That's what I see when I read Proverbs 31. She was simply growing and thriving where she was.

Where are you at today on the issue of discontentment? Is this scarf of blue making you feel blue?

*Today's assignment is to write out your perfect day. As a Christian woman, desiring to live for God, what would your perfect day look like?

Let it out. Hold nothing back. God knows what you are thinking already!

After you've penned everything you believe will improve your life, review it and commit it to the Lord. Does your idea of living perfectly match His plan for you? Just as He spoke to me that morning, regarding my discontentment, I know He will speak to you. Take the time to listen. And whatever He is telling your dissatisfied heart, write it across the pages of your perfect day.

Perhaps it is simply, "Love Me and love others." Or perhaps it is something He has reserved just for you.

I love you, Dear Sisters, and I will see you back here for Day Two.

Journal…

_____

_____

_____

_____

_____

_____

_____

_____

_____

_____

_____

Father of Discontentment

"Discontent is like ink poured into water, which fills the whole fountain full of blackness. It casts a cloud over the mind, and renders it more occupied about the evil which disquiets than about the means of removing it." –Owen Feltham

"Satan is ever seeking to inject that poison into our hearts to distrust God's goodness - especially in connection with his commandments. That is what really lies behind all evil, lusting and disobedience. A discontent with our position and portion, a craving from something which God has wisely held from us. Reject any suggestion that God is unduly severe with you. Resist with the utmost abhorrence anything that causes you to doubt God's love and his loving-kindness toward you. Allow nothing to make you question the Father's love for his child." -A.W. Pink

These quotes are a good reminder of the poisonous effects discontentment can have on our lives and we must never forget the place where discontentment originated. Lucifer, a.k.a. Satan, was created as a beautiful angel, high in rank and adorned with jewels. But it was not enough for him. Discontentment entered his heart and eventually destroyed him.

*Please read Isaiah 14:12-15, and Ezekiel 28:11-15

The King James Version says, *"How art thou fallen from heaven, O Lucifer, son of the morning! How art thou cut down to the ground, which didst weaken the nations!"*

Although Ezekiel 28 is a lament concerning the King of Tyre, it also describes Lucifer as being the model of perfection, full of wisdom, perfect in beauty. In the Garden of Eden, he was adorned with precious stones such as: ruby, topaz, and emerald. He was also anointed as guardian cherub.

But it was not enough. In Satan's dissatisfaction, arrogance and pride, he took matters into his own hands, scorning what God had given him. Ladies, what has God given us? Do you know that the Bible says He has given us *everything* we need for life?

*Please read 2 Peter 1:3-4

Let's take a close look at these two verses. They are crucial for us as we deal with our scarf of discontentment.

Verse 3 reminds us of what He gave when we came to the saving knowledge of Jesus Christ. *His divine power* gave us everything we need, by His own glory and goodness.

The very same Spirit Who raised Jesus, the One promised to us in John chapter 16, resides in us!

What a powerful message for us Sisters! What an assurance it ought to be for our restless souls.
When Peter speaks of the "very great and precious promises," do we understand what he is saying?

Last Spring, I co-lead a study by Sheila Walsh, called "The Shelter of God's Promises." And I have to say it was one of the most beautiful studies I've ever participated in. You see, before the study, I had no clue what God's promises really were. I knew I had the promise of heaven because of my faith in Jesus, but beyond that I had no grasp of His great and precious promises.

Can you relate? Or do you have His promises deep in your heart?

*Today, I want you to write down every promise from God that you know. I hope it is more than what I knew. I pray you will fill the entire journal page!

But no matter how many promises you write down, I want to remind you that the promises of God are too numerous to count! He truly has given us everything we need for life and godliness.

*After you write out the promises you already know, let me challenge you to find one more from the Scriptures that you didn't know before. Pray, seek and find what the Lord has promised to those who love Him. See you for Week Three.

Journal...

_____

_____

_____

_____

_____

_____

_____

Godliness with Contentment...

In our last session together I gave a personal testimony of how God transformed my thinking one night, on the beach in Cancun. He reminded me of the cross and the ultimate sacrifice Jesus made so I could spend eternity with Him.

When I got home from that trip I was determined to live a life of gratitude.

Now, one of the things I had been unhappy with was my kitchen floor. It is still the original linoleum from 1982, brown, dull, ripped in places...and downright ugly.

But on that plane ride back to Denver, I made up my mind that I was going to treat that floor as if it were the prettiest tile I'd ever had. I mopped that ugly little floor until it shone. I ignored the flaws in it. I *thanked* God that we even had a floor. And you know what? Eventually, I forgot all about my discontentment concerning the kitchen floor! I figure that if and when the Lord provides the means for us to remodel, I will be extra appreciative. But for now, I will be thankful for my '82 linoleum and move on to more important things.

Sisters that is what God does for us! He changes our dissatisfaction to satisfaction-in Him alone.

So what is the key to finding that deep and lasting contentment even in the midst of unpleasant circumstances?

Take a look…

"I am the True Vine and my Father is the Gardener. He cuts off every branch in Me that bears no fruit, while every branch that does bear fruit He prunes so that it will be even more fruitful. You are already clean because of the word I have spoken to you. Remain in Me, and I will remain in you. No branch can bear fruit by itself; it must remain in the Vine. Neither can you bear fruit unless you remain in Me. I am the Vine; you are the branches. If a man remains in Me and I in him, he will bear much fruit; **apart** *from Me you can do nothing." John 15:1-5*

Like a pear tree that blossoms but never produces pears, we may be living Christian lives but not bearing much fruit. Why? Because discontentment leads us away from the Vine, causing us to take off in different directions.

Remember, Jesus said that apart from Him we can do nothing. But as discontented girls we are doing plenty! Always searching for something to fill the void, make us happier, and give us what we don't have, we end up like a wild olive-shoot growing in all kinds of directions but never producing a harvest.

Sisters, if there is only one word you will commit to memory for this issue, let it be ABIDE. Abide in Jesus not only for this season but for all seasons. When we feel discontentment rising in our hearts, and we want to put on that blue scarf…ABIDE.

Do we believe He can change our 'want to'?

Do we believe He can make our 1982 linoleum acceptable?

Do we believe He wants to give us the desire of our hearts according to His perfect will?

To close out this week, let's end with Scripture.

*Please read 1Timothy 6:6-10

Godliness with contentment is great gain…Godliness with contentment is great gain…*And one more time*…Godliness with contentment is great gain!

This verse does not only apply to money. It applies to every area of our lives. It applies to our desires for more talent, a different job, nicer things, a different house, etc.

Today Ladies, let's make a decision to discard the blue scarf. Jesus, the True Vine, is our satisfaction.

He so longs to produce abundant fruit in you! Will you lean in to Him? Remain? Wait upon Him? Abide?

*On your journal pages, make a commitment to be content with whatever you have and wherever you are today. Thank Him. Praise Him. Write down your commitment to *abide* in Him. Then, go and clean your kitchen floor with the biggest smile of contended freedom you've ever had!

Can't wait to see you for Week Four.

Journal…

∽ Homework Discussion Questions ∽

Week Three: Discontentment

(To be shared at the beginning of Week Four)

1. As you wrote out what your perfect day would look like, what insights did you gain into the issue of discontentment? What did you sense from the Lord?
2. What is your opinion on the Proverbs 31 woman? Was she perfect?
3. The Lord promises to provide everything we need. What about things we *want*?
4. What promises did you find from the Bible that you didn't know before?
5. Any other thoughts on the issue of discontentment?

Looking Ahead

"For God did not give us a spirit of timidity, but a spirit of power, of love and of self-discipline." 2 Timothy 1:7

Jennifer Waddle

～Four～
Scarf of Yellow...*Insecurity*

Inward Battle

Tell me if this rings a bell. Ten people congratulate you on a job well done, but *one* person has something negative to say and *that* is what you focus on. Sound familiar? Insecurity can zap our strength, put out our fire, hold us back, and ultimately cause us to be ineffective for Christ.

Take a look at the word I-n-s-e-c-u-r-e. The first two letters say a lot..."in" or "inward." When we struggle with insecurity, we think we are meek and humble and maybe even a victim, but really we are consumed with Me, Myself and I.

I'm not trying to be harsh. It's just that I've realized being insecure is really a form of self-centeredness. And believe me, I used to be the queen of insecurity!

When I was writing this study, I wanted to know what the Bible said about insecurity. I knew that if I could understand it from a Biblical perspective, there would be a chance to not only overcome it, but help others to do the same. The actual word isn't expressed in the Bible, but one man's experience portrayed intense insecurity and divine help from the Lord.

Pray with me as we open our hearts to the Word of God.

"Lord, we come before You, each with our own insecurities. But we are reminded that You are our loving Creator and that you created each of us in Your image...Your image! Thank you, Father, for designing each of us to fulfill a purpose for Your glory. Help us to keep our focus on You and not on self. We desire to be free from our insecurities and confident in Your Son, Jesus Christ. It is in His name we pray...amen."

*Please read Exodus 4:1-16.

If this is not the crown example of insecurity, I don't know what is. Moses, the one chosen by the **Great I Am** to go to Pharaoh, doubted and worried and fretted until the Lord's anger burned against him. Even with the miracles God performed right there on the spot, Moses couldn't stop thinking about his own limitations.

Now we see from the text that God was ultimately merciful to Moses by sending Aaron to be his mouthpiece. But that was not the original plan. God wanted *Moses* to do it.

The Lord said to him, *"Who gave man his mouth? Who makes him deaf or mute? Who gives him sight or makes him blind? Is it not I, the Lord? Now go; I will help you speak and will teach you what to say."(Exodus 4:11-12)*

Sisters, if God has called us, He will help us. Remember, He is the Potter and we are the clay. He made us. He equips us.

"Yet, O Lord, You are our Father. We are the clay, You are the Potter; we are all the work of Your hand."(Isaiah 64:8)

"I praise You because I am fearfully and wonderfully made; Your works are wonderful, I know that full well." (Psalm 139:14)

We have probably heard these verses many times, but do we believe them? Perhaps we believe them about others but not ourselves.

Looking back, I have pretty good memories of grade school, in the little Kansas town where I grew up. I had great teachers in the third and fourth grades. But by the time I reached Jr. High, I had become the target of a group of mean girls. I specifically remember a time in the seventh grade when a girl pushed me up against a brick wall and pulled me up by my shirt collar. Face to face with this tall red-head, the only thing I could think to do was say something funny. And luckily for me it worked! I don't even remember what I said, but after a few seconds she laughed and let me go.

The ninth and tenth grades were worse as I moved into High School. A burly senior, with beady eyes, locked me and my best friend in the gym lockers. But the most damaging type of bullying I endured was the *constant criticism* of who I was. During those impressionable years, I grew to believe I was worthless. And you know how I handled it? I did everything I could to prove them wrong.

Cheerleading, volleyball, choir, band, drama, student council…were some of the things I strove for, in an attempt for acceptance and approval from my peers. I was scared to death of failure because I had come to believe that was exactly what I was.

As you can guess, insecurity was one of the darkest forces in my life for many, many years. It didn't really hold me back from trying things, but it turned my focus to *desperately seeking man's approval*... a very dangerous path.

For some, insecurity paralyzes them so they cannot or will not invest the gifts and talents God has given them. They self-criticize, hold back, and miss out on some of God's plans for them.

Ladies, I truly don't believe insecurity is only a matter of self-esteem or scars from having been mistreated. Yes, those play a role. We learn things that we have to unlearn. But Sisters, we have to come to terms with the fact that insecurity about who we are is a rejection of the Potter's hand.

That is a tough concept. Our insecurity has made us feel like victims, and it is difficult to imagine it being a sinful issue in our lives. And I hope you know I say all of this with great love for you. I know what it feels like to be rejected, teased, and criticized until I felt like pond scum. And that, my friends is not easy to overcome. I am not trying to diminish your pain, but I am wanting to magnify the God of the Universe who has called us to bring Him glory!

Insecurity does not magnify the Lord. It turns the magnifying glass toward ourselves and says, look at me. Woe is me. Poor me.

Most of all, it hinders our walk with the Lord. We become like Moses, where we doubt and argue and beg for God to call someone else when He has chosen *us*.

I don't want to forsake the call of God because of fear or doubt or insecurity. I want to be so focused on Him that I will obey.

And when I am afraid or uncertain, I want to quickly deal with it by going to Him and asking for strength, clarity and help.

I realize that insecurity doesn't go away easily, especially if it is a habit for us. But this week we are going to face this scarf of yellow. We are going to recognize it for what it is and we are going to use God's truth to conquer it.

We are going to look at the life of Gideon, a man of great potential, but plagued with insecurity.

We are going to put on "Christ-confidence," not self-confidence.

And, we are going to be challenged to step out in faith concerning what God is calling us to do.

It is going to be a very exciting week and I am praying with all my heart that you will return with wonderful stories of success!

Yellow-Bellied Girls

Watch any of the Old Westerns and you will probably hear the term 'Yellow-Belly.' A slang term for cowardice, the cowboy spits in the dirt, adjusts his hat and says with a snarl, "You're just a yellow-bellied lizard without a tail."

In my research, I came across a website of "Western Slang and Old West Insults." I laughed out loud at some of the silly phrases. Here are some of the best ones I found. (Bear with me!)

"He's so crooked, he could swallow nails and spit out corkscrews."

"His mustache smelled like a mildewed saddle blanket after it had been rid on a sore back hoss, three hundred miles in August."

"He had a ten-dollar Stetson on a five-cent head."

"His family tree was a shrub."

Funny, huh? Makes me want to wear a cowboy hat and kick the dirt. But all joking aside, I seriously have to ask…

What are we so afraid of?

Let's spend some time in the Scriptures today and see a clear example of insecurity.

*Please read Judges 6:7-40

Gideon, whose name means "cutter of trees," lived in the time when Israel was ravaged by the Midianites and other people groups. The Midianites ruined their crops, did not spare their livestock, and swarmed Israel like a band of locusts.

In the middle of all this, Gideon was called to be the fifth judge of Israel. There was no king or ruler and Israel was once again in big trouble.

The first mention of Gideon places him in the *winepress* threshing wheat. He was hiding from the Midianites. Now do we blame him? No. They had to eat; they had to survive; and threshing wheat in the winepress was a way to protect what little they had left.

But Gideon's fear and insecurity was so intense, he questioned and doubted everything the Lord told him. And it surprises me that God was so patient. After all, remember how the Lord's anger burned against Moses?

But remember…*the Lord is slow to anger and abounding in love*. And He understands fully our tendencies toward insecurity. Now, I do not want us to assume it is ok to question our Maker over and over, and ask for signs. There is something to be said for walking in faith even when we don't understand it all.

Gideon had it in his mind that because he was from the weakest clan and the least in his family, the Lord certainly could not be visiting him, could not be calling him to be the judge of Israel.

The Lord said, *"Go in the strength you have…am I not sending you?"*

Isn't that beautiful? ***"Go in the strength you have…"***

We think we know our limitations better than anyone, but only our Maker knows every fiber of our being.

Gideon did carry out the Lord's plans. He did defeat the Midianites. However, when I read his account, I am reminded of my own battle with fear and insecurity. I can relate to Gideon far more than I'd like to admit. I have been guilty of doubting God and asking for proof of His will over and over. And I sometimes worry that He will become weary of me.

Ever feel that way?

Let me give y'all a pep-talk for a minute. We are not…I re-peat…*not*…yellow-bellied girls. We are women of valor, equipped with the armor of God. We can go. We can do. We can be exactly who He created us to be!

Sisters, we must throw off everything that hinders and the sin that so easily entangles. Insecurity must go. These yellow scarves aren't pretty. They are *petty.*

*So as we close today, your assignment is to do something bold for Christ. Please don't tune me out. I want you to stop and think about the very thing God is calling you to do and I want you to take the first step in doing it.

Do you need to make a phone call? Send an e-mail? Meet someone face to face? Accept a position? Whatever it is that you have so insecurely put aside, I want you to commit it to the Lord and go do it!

Write it down so you won't forget the bold step you took on this very day.

The Lord is with you! The One and Only God of the Universe is with *you.*

So put your boots on and fasten those spurs. Grab the reigns and hang on tight. I cannot wait to hear of your courage this week!

Journal...

✝ Week Four Homework/Day Two

The Best Kind of Confidence

Of all the ladies I spoke with during the writing of this study, insecurity was the number one issue. And it really is no laughing matter. Insecurity manifests itself in different ways. It can show up as fear, defensiveness, pride, and self-centeredness. It can also be a very debilitating issue.

Yesterday we took a look at the life of Gideon and God's extreme patience with him.

Today we will read about a beautiful example of uncertainty in the face of severe trial, and perfect obedience in spite of it.

Please read Matthew 26:36-46

Sisters, we do not even understand the amount of sorrow, fear, and perhaps insecurity Jesus must have been faced with. It makes me ashamed to think I am insecure about stepping out in faith, when my Savior was faced with something I will never fully comprehend.

Jesus' final response when they came to arrest Him was, *"Friend, do what you came for."*

How could He go from being overwhelmed to the point of death, to simply surrendering?

Because of His confidence in the cross, and the salvation it would bring for all who would receive Him, He was able to conquer any fear or insecurity.

Sisters, we don't need more self-confidence. We don't need higher self-esteem. We don't need any more of *self*, thank you very much.

But we desperately need Christ-confidence. Confidence in knowing that what He did on the cross is enough of a reason to step out of our comfort zones and boldly live for Him!

"Let us fix our eyes on Jesus, the Author and Perfecter of our faith, Who for the joy set before Him endured the cross, scorning its shame, and sat down at the right hand of the throne of God. Consider Him Who endured such opposition from sinful men so that you will not grow weary and lose heart." Hebrews 12:2-3

Dear ones, what opposition are you facing? What is keeping this scarf of insecurity firmly around your neck?

Today I want you to find that quiet place…a place with no distractions. I want you to fix your eyes upon Jesus. Acknowledge Him as the Author and Perfecter of your faith. Remember Him today. Remember that He endured the cross for your sake. Thank Him. Really thank Him.

And as you consider the opposition He faced, opposition leading to his crucifixion, let the reality of that put your insecurity into perspective. Our fears don't seem so big in light of the cross do they?

I am praying for Christ-confidence to cover us today, as we let the yellow scarf fall to the floor. After all, *His* confidence is the best kind to have.

Love you, Dear Sisters…see you back for Day Three.

Journal…

Jennifer Waddle

✟ Week Four Homework/Day Three

What do I Know to be true?

We've done some intensive work on our issue of insecurity, and I hope you are beginning to see some changes. We have stepped out in faith. We have replaced self-confidence for Christ-confidence. And I pray you are growing more and more secure in the Lord's plan for your life.

Often times, when I begin to doubt, I go back to what I *know* is true. For example, I was recently asked to speak for a big event and initially I was thrilled. But, as I should have known, the devil came in to steal that joy and replace it with insecurity.

What started out as an answer to prayer, became a sea of doubt that maybe I hadn't heard the Lord correctly.

I had to ask myself, "What do I KNOW to be true?"

1. I *knew* that I had prayed for opportunity to share God's Word with other women.
2. I *knew* that the Lord had given me a desire to encourage.
3. I *knew* that the event would bring Him glory and His Word would not return void.

Sisters, in this area of insecurity we need to have regular pep-talks with ourselves. What do you *know* to be true?

Ephesians 2:10 says, ***"For we are God's workmanship, created in Christ Jesus to do good works, which God prepared in advance for us to do."***

We know this verse! But do we believe it?

I realize we may get nervous or jittery when we step out in faith. After all, we are only human. But insecurity can be debilitating. It can stop us from being active participants in God's workmanship and cause us to be complacent and ineffective for Christ.

Let's get into the Word and get some security around our necks rather than these pathetic, yellow scarves.

*Please read Joshua 1:6-9

What more would we ever need than to know that the Lord our God is with us? In every moment of every day, every month of every year, He will be with us wherever we go.

*On your journal pages, write three verses that you can proclaim in the moment of doubt. Spend time in the Scriptures and let the Lord speak to your fearful heart. Write the verses down. Memorize them. Carry them with you. You will need them in the days to come. The scarf of insecurity will always try to make its way back into our dresser drawer, but each time we see it, we will say, "No thanks," and keep going.

I am looking forward to hearing the verses you find. We all need them as encouragement to keep the faith!

I'll see you soon for Week Five of our study.

Journal…

Jennifer Waddle

∽ Homework Discussion Questions ∽

Week Four: Insecurity

(To be shared at the beginning of Week Five)

1. Reading about the life of Gideon, we learned that he stepped out in bold faith despite his insecurity. What bold thing is God calling you to do?
2. Do you believe there was a level of insecurity when Jesus prayed in the Garden of Gethsemane? What does it mean to have Christ-Confidence instead of Self-Confidence?
3. What verses did you find that you can use to combat doubt, fear, or insecurity?
4. Any other thoughts on the issue of insecurity?

Looking Ahead

"When pride comes, then comes disgrace, but with humility comes wisdom." Proverbs 11:2

∼Five∼
Scarf of Purple...*Pride*

Lady Pride

The color purple, in the Bible, stands for royalty. The Proverbs 31 woman was clothed in fine linen and purple. Lydia, of the New Testament, sold purple garments. And King Solomon included purple into the veil of the temple. Purple is rich and beautiful, and symbolizes ornamental grace.

Look at these interesting facts from history:

Some Native Americans view purple as a sign of wisdom.
In Japan it symbolizes wealth and power.
In Egypt it can be a sign of virtue and faith.
Here in America we honor soldiers with the purple heart of bravery.
Ancient Rome allowed only emperors and magistrates to wear the color purple. Any other uses of it was punishable by death.
And here is a random one...The planet Jupiter is sometimes referred to as the purple planet.

For our issue of pride, I chose purple to symbolize the self-designated royalty of our thoughts and attitudes.

Picture with me, for a minute, "Lady Pride." She holds her head high and looks down her nose at others. Judgment is usually her first reaction. She is critical, hard to please, and easily offended. Impatience is often a part of her wardrobe.

Proverbs says that *pride comes before a fall.* Maybe it's because Lady Pride is so focused on keeping her head held high, she doesn't see the dip in the road. Down she goes, eventually, for the scarf of pride can only be worn so long.

As we deal with our scarves of purple, I just want to say that all of us struggle with pride in one way or another. For some of us it is a passing moment and we take it to God and move on. But for others, it is a persistent sin issue. We may not even realize how ingrained pride is, until the fall comes.

I want us to look at King Hezekiah from the Old Testament and how pride slipped in…pride that would eventually reap destruction.

*Please read 2 Kings 20:1-19

Hezekiah was shown great mercy by God and given fifteen more years to live and reign. However, the enemy swooped in, pouncing on the opportunity.

Ladies, he knew exactly who the gift bearing messengers were. Babylon had been around since Genesis and the tower of Babel. Known for its ruthless and domineering ways, the visit should have been a major red flag for Hezekiah.

I find it interesting that when Isaiah asked him where the messengers were from, Hezekiah first said, *"From a distant land…"*

Do you suppose he was trying to soften the hard truth that they were from Babylon?

However, Hezekiah's next statement is very brazen, as if he suddenly lost all pretense.

*"They saw everything in my palace. There is nothing among **my** treasures I did not show them."* (Emphasis mine)

My treasures…hmm…

Isaiah answered him. ***"The time will surely come when everything in your palace, and all that your fathers have stored up until this day, will be carried off to Babylon."***

Sisters, Hezekiah's prideful actions would have dire consequences. *Seventy years* of Babylonian captivity and the destruction of the temple, as well as Jerusalem, would be the outcome of this prideful act.

Jeremiah 9:23-24 says, ***This is what the Lord says,** **"Let not the wise man boast of his wisdom or the strong man boast of his strength or the rich man boast of his riches, but let him who boasts boast about this: that he understands and knows Me, that I am the Lord who exercises kindness, justice and righteousness on earth, for in these I delight."***

Ladies, as we learn more this week, I am going to ask that you dig deep, to the root of any pride issues in your life. As much as I would like to say I don't have a problem with pride, I cannot.

In fact, not long ago, I was taken off guard with a bout of pride that really shook me up. It happened at a Praise Team meeting where our Worship Pastor had called all instrumentalists together for an evening of practice. Three of us keyboardists showed up. The other two are friends of mine who I care for very much.

I specifically remember Justin sitting all of us down; all the guitar players, drummers, etc., and saying, "Tonight, we are going to have to leave our pride at the door and simply learn from one another."
I thought to myself, *No problem. I don't have any pride to leave at the door.*

Tsk, tsk, tsk…

I should have known the enemy would pounce on that opportunity. Within minutes I was battling all sorts of pride issues in my mind. The other 2 keyboardist were asked to play first and I found myself sitting on the sidelines. I tried to pray, tried to sing along, tried everything to get the "woe is me" thoughts out of my mind. I struggled for the entire two hour practice! My pride kept me from being able to worship. It kept me from learning. Ultimately, it got the best of me. I went home and complained to my husband Jim, who had the wisdom to tell me to sleep on it and see how I felt in the morning.

Sure enough, by morning I was over it. In fact, I felt humbled and sorry for the way I had reacted. I had missed out on a wonderful time of praise and worship and learning from my friends because of pride.
This week, we are going to see various facets of pride and how harmful it really is. Anyone who knows a prideful person can agree that their behavior is most unpleasant to be around.

We need to get this scarf off of our necks and discarded in the trash. It is not flattering to us at all. It is not a sign of royalty for us. It is about as ugly as a scarf can be.

I don't know about you, but if pride really does come before a fall, then I want to take it off now before I crash and burn. How about you? Let's pray…

"Lord of Heaven, we bow before You today, laying our crowns at Your feet. O Lord how we need a dose of humility. Our pride is like a terrible stench to You, for You alone are exalted. Forgive us God for lifting our heads high and looking down on others. Forgive us for the judgmental thoughts that come so easily. We know that You call us to love one another and to not see ourselves more highly than we ought. We need Your wisdom and instruction this week. Thank You Lord, for hearing us. We remain humble and teachable as Your Word changes our prideful hearts. In Jesus' name, amen."

✝ Week Five Homework/Day One:

Powerless Pride

Have you ever had to pull weeds? If you haven't, then blessed art thou among women!

I know I have pulled a fair amount of weeds in my life, and it's not so bad as long as the roots come up easily. But some weeds are so stubborn, the tops break off leaving the root. And soon the weed is back.

I think our issues of pride are like that. We know in our hearts when we are letting conceit or a 'holier than thou' attitude creep in. But until we get to the root of it, pride will linger just beneath the surface, and before long, raise its ugly head.

There is a passage in the book of Hosea that first gives us the solution to pride, then the dilemma. Take a look.

*Please read Hosea 10:12-13

Now if you aren't familiar with this Old Testament book, I highly encourage you to study it for yourselves. The command God gave Hosea, to take an adulterous wife, is a command that not many would have the strength to carry out. What does this have to do with our issue of pride? Let's look closely at our passage.

First, we are given the solution. *"Sow yourselves to righteousness, reap in mercy, and break up your fallow ground. Seek the Lord until He comes and rains righteousness upon you."(NKJV)*

Then, the hard truth… *"You have plowed wickedness, reaped iniquity, eaten the fruit of lies, trusted in your own way and in the multitude of your mighty men." (NKJV)*

I have no doubt that Hosea was the perfect prophet for the Kingdom of Israel in his time.

He was chosen to be a living example, and to announce judgment on Israel for being unfaithful to God. They were sacrificing to Baal. They were full of lies and murder, theft and adultery. And they were stumbling in their pride.

I love the word picture in our passage that indicates sowing and reaping.

On one hand, we must uproot pride. But on the other, we must allow ourselves be sown into righteousness. Look at it this way…

When a seed is sown, it is basically tossed to the ground, and lies in great peril. Exposed and vulnerable in the dirt, the seed remains in the hot sun, and is at risk of being blown away by the wind. But at *just the right time,* the Sower gives it much needed water and tender care. Then it takes root.

Hosea reminds us to sow ourselves to righteousness. This is not to be confused with self-righteousness, but a *laying down of self.* Throwing ourselves at the feet of Jesus, in the dirt, in the hot sun, in the wind, and letting Him break up the fallow ground, is the only way to fully humble ourselves. Yes, pride must always be uprooted, but in its place, righteousness must always be sown.

Sisters, why does pride have such deep, stubborn roots? Because there is an awful, uncomfortable feeling of vulnerability when we take off the purple scarf. Without it, we are left exposed to weakness.

Like Superman, when he is just plain old Clark Kent, we feel weak. With the cape, he can fly around the world a hundred times in a minute. But without it he is nerdy, awkward, and *powerless.*

Ahh…the "P" word…powerless, that's the root isn't it? We hate feeling powerless. We don't want anyone to know we are weak, or fallible or anything less than perfect.

But God…oh the wonders of God!

"You see, at just the right time, when we were still powerless, Christ died for the ungodly." (Rom. 5:6)

Jesus didn't sacrifice Himself on our behalf because we had it all together and were doing everything right. *While we were still powerless,* lost, hopeless, ungodly and full of sin, Christ died for us.

Ladies, only by the Holy Spirit of God can we stand! The scarf of pride gives us a false sense of power and control, but is nothing but a man-made cover for our frailty.

The rest of Hosea is full of rich verses that explain not only Israel's tendency to wander from God, but also explains our tendencies toward pride.

"It was I who taught Ephraim to walk, taking them by the arms; but they did not realize it was I who healed them." (Hosea 11:3)

"Ephraim boasts, 'I am very rich; I have become wealthy. With all my wealth they will not find in me any iniquity or sin.'" (Hosea 12:8)

"When I fed them, they were satisfied; when they were satisfied they became proud; then they forgot me." (Hosea 13:6)

We are so forgetful aren't we?

We quickly forget Who saved us from our sinful selves. We forget it was the Lord Who taught us how to walk, after we were born again. We forget that every good and perfect gift comes from above.

"Lord Jesus, help us in our issue of pride! We know, O Lord that you humble those who exalt themselves, but you lift up those who are humble. We surrender ourselves to You. As a seed lying on the ground, waiting to grow, Lord we bow before You. We love You and wait for Your righteousness to fall on us. In Jesus' name, amen."

Sisters, it is time for us to break up the fallow ground. Nothing good can grow unless we break through the hard exterior of pride.

*Today's assignment is to make a list of areas where you have trusted in your own way. Above God, above your spouse, above those in authority over you, when has it been difficult to submit? When have you held your head so high you could see no other way?

Perhaps you have walked in pride so long it is difficult to pin-point specific things. But you know in your heart there is an unhealthy sense of self-confidence that has no place in the Christian life; a self-confidence that has raised itself above Christ-confidence.

I am with you in this, and praying hard for the Lord to rain down His righteousness upon all of us. See you for Day Two.

Journal...

A Head Taller...

Yesterday we had the tough assignment of writing down our stubborn areas of pride. I hope you were able to complete the assignment. The sooner we open up about it, the sooner we can deal with it. As women, I think it is easy to cover up pride so that no one will notice. But God notices. He really does.

King Saul in the Old Testament is a very prominent example of someone who consistently let pride overtake him. I wish we had the time and fortitude to read all of 1Samuel, but for our study we will highlight Saul's life and his issue of pride.

*Please read 1Samuel 9:1-17

Saul's outward appearance was one of seeming nobility, at least according to the world. The Bible says he was impressive and without equal...a head taller than the other Israelites.

Now I do not think taller is better. In fact, my long-time friend Rebecca is barely five foot tall, and she is one of the strongest girls I know. We used to work out together on a regular basis and boy could she out-lift, out-run, out-do me in everything! I would be huffing and puffing and complaining the whole time, while she would bench press twice as much. Tiny, but tough. That's my friend!

But Saul stood out among the young men. And God chose him to be the first king of Israel. Now, in the beginning, Saul didn't seem to struggle with pride.

*Please read 1 Samuel 9:21

This verse reminds me of old Gideon! Saul, too, was convinced Samuel had the wrong person. No pride there. But let's jump ahead in 1 Samuel.

*Please read 1 Samuel 13:1-14

Now in my limited understanding of the culture, it seems to me that Saul's actions weren't so bad. So he blew the trumpet and shouted, "Let the Hebrews hear!" Was that a sign of pride? Not necessarily. But the fact that he loudly announced his achievements, points to a very different Saul than we read about in chapter nine.

When Samuel did not come at the set time, Saul took it upon himself to sacrifice the burnt offering. His excuse was that he wanted to seek the Lord's favor, but the hard truth was, he thought he could take Samuel's place, and by doing so he failed to keep the Lord's command.

Sisters, we too fail to keep God's commands when we think we know better. We get tired of waiting, and in our pride we think we can handle it.

Unfortunately, Saul's issue of pride got a lot worse.

*Please Read 1Samuel 18:6-9

Young, handsome, rock throwing David had entered the picture. And the women noticed! They came out dancing and singing and playing tambourines.

"Saul has slain his thousands, and David his tens of thousands."

Anger, jealousy and pride overcame Saul, to the point that he tried to kill David. The Bible also says that Saul was afraid of David because he had God's favor.

David wounded Saul's pride by simply being a man after God's own heart. How much better off would Saul have been if he too sought to be such a man?

Ladies, pride is a huge distraction from living as a daughter of God. Pride over what we have or what we can achieve stands in the way of being women after His own heart.

*Today, I would like you to write down what exactly you are striving for. Recognition? Approval? Notoriety? Achievement? Success? Power? Is there anything someone else is doing that you would like to do? That you think you might be better at?

Tough stuff, I know. But honesty is going to be the best policy here. We may find that the things we are striving for aren't bad in and of themselves, but our prideful attitudes are. We need to bring everything under the authority of Christ Jesus. We can hold nothing back.

Hang in there, Sisters. I will see you for Day Three.

Journal…

Humble Beginnings

No one likes to be humiliated. It is a terrible feeling and can cause great pain. When a child is humiliated instead of instructed, the parent might get the response they desire, but they are really planting roots of anger, bitterness and a defense mechanism of pride.

Our God is not in the humiliating business. But He is in the *humility* business.

Look at these Proverbs regarding humility:

"When pride comes, then comes disgrace, but with humility comes wisdom." Prov. 11:2

"The fear of the Lord teaches a man wisdom, and humility comes before honor." Prov. 15:33

"Before his downfall a man's heart is proud, but humility comes before honor." Prov. 18:12

"Humility and the fear of the Lord bring wealth and honor and life." Prov. 22:4

The word *honor* is used in three of the four verses above, and isn't that what a prideful person most desires?

Pride makes us desperate to be honored, but it is in *humility* that the honor comes. How can this be?

A story is told about Mother Theresa, the nun who came from very humble beginnings and began her ministry by reaching out to the dying people of Calcutta, India. She did not seek fame or honor, but as she continued in a life of deep humility and sacrifice to serve others, she became well-known around the world.

Eventually, she was invited to Washington D.C. as an honored guest at a luncheon. In the book, Sacred Stories, by Ruth Tucker, one U.S. Senator's wife, Dee Jepson, described the event well.

"In came this tiny woman, even smaller than I had expected, wearing that familiar blue and white habit, over it a gray sweater that had seen many better days, which she wore again to the White House the next day. As that little woman walked into the room, her bare feet in worn sandals, I saw some of the most powerful leaders in this country stand to their feet with tears in their eyes just to be in her presence."

Mother Theresa's humility came before honor. She didn't seek it, or ask for it, or probably even recognize it, but it was given none-the-less.

Ladies, no matter what we are seeking, the scarf of pride has to go. There is absolutely no place for it in the Christian life. It can bring no good.

Do you struggle with this issue? Do you know someone who does? Pray right now for deliverance.

And can I suggest that we practice letting others see our weaknesses? Can I encourage us to wear the same worn-out old sweater to the White House? Figuratively speaking, we need a dose of that kind of humility.

*So far this week, we have written out areas where we have trusted ourselves even more than God. We have penned our desires for success and achievement. But today, I want us to get lower than low. Go to that secret and quiet place where you are *completely alone with the Lord*. No media, no distraction.

Get on you faces, Dear Sisters. Humble yourselves before the Lord. Expose your every weakness unto Him. And as you do, let the peace of God wash over you, assuring you that He is God and there is no other. Give Him all the glory and honor you have been seeking for yourself. Let any thoughts of performance or self-righteousness fade away. Be completely vulnerable to His presence.

After your quiet time, please write a prayer of humility. Start with, "Lord, I come humbly before You…"

May the Lord bless you in this. May He lift you up in due time. And may you finally release the scarf of pride into His hands.

I look forward to seeing you for Week Six.

∼ Homework Discussion Questions ∼

Week Five: Pride

(To be shared at the beginning of Week Six)

1. You were asked to write down areas where you have trusted in your own way. Would you like to share?
2. If there are things in this life we are striving for, such as promotion, recognition, achievement, etc., how can we keep these from being prideful acts?
3. If you completed the 'prayer of humility,' what things were you led to write down?
4. Any other thoughts on the issue of pride?

Looking Ahead

"Arise, Lord! Lift up Your hand, O God. Do not forget the helpless...But You, O God, do see trouble and grief; You consider it to take it in hand. The victim commits himself to you; You are the helper of the fatherless." (Psalm 10:12&14)

"...for a little while you may have had to suffer grief in all kinds of trials. These have come so that your faith, of greater worth than gold, which perishes even though refined by fire, may be proved genuine and may result in praise, glory and honor when Jesus Christ is revealed." (1Peter 1:6-7)

~Six~
Scarf of Black…*Oppression*

Just Beyond the Storm

As we are nearing the end of our study, we come face to face with the most difficult scarves of all. You know this scarf by name. It is unique to you. This garment resembles something so difficult to conquer, you wonder if it is even possible. The black scarf may symbolize grief, loneliness, depression, addiction, or un-forgiveness. It is unwelcome and unwanted, but still it remains in the confines of your heart.

Perhaps this scarf ended up in your drawer unexpectedly. Like a tornado, your life was rocked to the core and pain was wrapped around your neck without warning.

Sisters, may I take a moment to simply pray right now? Of all the issues we have discussed, this one is the most difficult. And my heart breaks for the many difficulties you are facing or have faced. Let's pray.

Almighty God, thank You. Yes Lord, thank You even in this, for Your ways are higher than ours. Lord, we need You. We need You more than ever before. We are hurting. But You know all about it. Our lives are in Your hands. Your Word says that You see our grief and You take it in hand. Thank You. Please cover us in Your peace today. Help us to see clearly Your will and Your way. We love You and trust You, in Jesus' Name. Amen.

As I write this, my heart is heavy with a burden so deep, it threatens to pull me under. My scarf of black is one of desperation. It is desperation for the very life of someone I love. It is so intensely bound around my neck that I have to remind myself to breathe.

What are you facing my Dear Sisters?

Of all the synonyms I found for the word oppression, such as: desolation, melancholy and unhappiness, the one that hit home was the word "heartsickness." Because no matter what deep-rooted issue this is, it makes our hearts sick.

Please don't misunderstand. I am in no way trying to gloss over any physical pain you may be going through. I know that I cannot even begin to understand some of the trials you have faced or are facing. But friend, in the middle of all the pain, amidst the turmoil, how is the condition of your heart?

I am asking myself the same question as I face this very serious time in my life. How is my heart?

A good friend used to ask me that all the time. We would call to catch up on each other's lives and she would always ask, "Jen, how is your heart?" I loved her for that. And even when I didn't have an answer for her, it always got me thinking.

Let's look at what the Bible has to say.

*Let's read Psalm 9:7-10, Psalm 12:5-6, and Psalm 72:4-5

From only three passages, we are given a multitude of truths. As I list them, pause to thank God for His true and unfailing love.

1. **He is our refuge when we are oppressed, a stronghold in times of trouble.**
2. **He does not forsake those who seek Him.**
3. **The Lord will arise and will protect us.**
4. **His words are flawless. We can fully trust them.**
5. **He will defend the afflicted.**
6. **He will save the children of the needy.**
7. **And the best of all...He will crush the oppressor!**

If you are like me, you read these truths and believe them, but you believe they will come true in the future. Right now seems too difficult. After all, the Scriptures indicate that God *will* not forsake us. He *will* rise to protect us. He *will* defend, and He *will* crush the enemy.

But what about right here and now? Sisters, *right now* He is our refuge. *Right now* He does not forsake us. *Right now* He arises to protect us. *Right now* we can fully trust Him.

Now, you may think I am strange, but I really like cloudy days. Gloomy days...rainy days...and especially blizzards make me happy. I have always gotten excited when the forecast says there is a big storm coming.

And as I ponder this, I realize that one reason I like stormy days is because they give me permission to be lazy. As terrible as it sounds, I like the fact that it is too yucky outside to get up and get going. I use cloudy, gloomy days as excuses to be a lazy bum.

When it comes to oppression I think we tend to follow the storm cloud. It eventually moves away from us but we follow it, stand under it, and use it as a sort of security blanket.

When I was eighteen years old, I was a foreign exchange student in Belgium. Now Belgium is a tiny country that sits below Holland, east of France, and west of Germany. It is very green and beautiful, but it rains *all of the time.* On average, it is rainy 132 days per year. And by the time I got half way through that school year, I was down-right depressed.

Ladies, that's how oppression works. It may hit us unexpectedly, like a storm, but the longer we are under it, the more down-and-out we become.

So what are we to do when the struggle is very real? When we have no power to blow the dark clouds away?

Look beyond the storm. There is blue sky above the rain.

I'd like to share some personal lyrics with you from a song called, "Just beyond the Storm."

The storm clouds are breaking, the sun is shining through
I can't even remember when I first lost sight of You
But now the rain is ceasing, the wind is on my face
Bringing with it perfect peace and Your incredible grace
I'm finished wandering, through this desert of testing
I'm ready to take Your hand as You take my heart...
You were right behind the clouds, just beyond the storm
Waiting patiently for me to lift up my arms
But every time You called my name, I just failed to see
Through the clouds and just beyond the storm...

Ladies, we all know that our Sovereign Lord is not behind any cloud or hidden from us in any way. But the scarf of oppression makes us think He is far off. The black cloud of despair does not change His faithfulness, but it makes us think it does.

This week we will learn to look at oppression through God's perspective. We will be given tools to get out from underneath the weight. And we will hopefully release the oppression once and for all.

Backpack of Bricks...

Oppression: the feeling of being heavily burdened by troubles.

In our session, we looked at several foundational truths about oppression. The Psalms gave us clear words of comfort and hope. But for most of us, the words were unable to penetrate deep into our hearts and minds because of the dark cloud that is hovering.

Today, we are going to stop and remember how it all began. What originally took place in our lives that eventually became a burden too heavy to carry?

Picture it this way...

Life was going along and you were doing just fine. But one day, you were given a backpack to wear. It was heavy, but not too heavy. The backpack was a trial. It was painful and burdensome, but you kept your chin up and kept moving forward in faith.

It was then that The Lord reminded you that His yoke was easy and His burden was light. He was giving you permission to take the backpack off...give it to Him. But you had gotten used to carrying it. It had become a part of you.

The faith that allowed you to move forward in the beginning, began to falter, and the backpack became heavier and heavier. It was as if bricks were being added one by one. And as time went by, you became more and more burdened. The original trial, *never more than you could bear,* became an unbearable weight of oppression.

You see, Satan will take any trial the Lord has allowed in our lives and turn it into the biggest, ugliest mess, so twisted and tangled, we feel as though we may never break free. And then he begins to add more and more weight until we are completely slumped over, barely able to put one foot in front of the other.

But God…

God in all His Sovereignty and Holiness does not permit us to remain in this state. It may seem impossible to be delivered from this yoke of oppression, but He is the Great Deliverer!

*Please read 2 Corinthians 1:3-10

What a poignant example of real hardship, immense pressure, and despair. But Paul made it clear they did not remain there. He insisted on relying completely on God, the Father of compassion and comfort. Sisters, whatever it was that started it all, whatever was in that original backpack, *it is possible to let it go.*

The popular Disney movie, Frozen, has that catchy song called "Let it Go." I hear kids singing it in the grocery store! And one line in the song says, "Can't hold it back anymore, let it go, let it go, turn away and slam the door."

Isn't it time to loosen the straps of the backpack you're carrying?

*Today's assignment is simply this…to make a list of the things that are in that backpack. Brick, by brick, what names are on them? Grief, loneliness, depression, un-forgiveness?

Write them down. Commit them to God. Pray, pray, pray. The Lord Your God is with you. We are one step closer to untying this scarf of black. I'll see you back here for Day Two.

Journal…

Baby Elephants...

Have you ever heard what happens to a baby elephant whose ankle has been chained to a post for a period of time? At first he tugs and pulls and longs to break free from the restraint. But after a while, he relents and surrenders to the fact that the chain will only allow him to circle the pen so far.

Then, the trainers can simply unhook the elephant from the post, leaving a loose chain around his ankle and he will still walk around as if he were bound. Why? Because he *has it in his mind* that he is still tied to the post.

Aren't we so like that elephant? I know I am. Jesus Christ released us from every tie, every bond and every chain. We are free to live for Him, yet we are limited to going round and round in circles because of our *trained minds.*

Oppression skews our vision of the truth. And Sisters, only the Truth can set us free.

*Please read John 14:1-4, 25-27

When Jesus says, *"Do not let your hearts be troubled,"* are we taking it as a suggestion or a command? And how can we avoid a troubled heart when heartache is very, very real?

I believe the Lord is telling us to trust. This may seem elementary, but when it comes to oppression we need the reminder to *trust Him.*

The baby elephant trusts that he can't leave the pen, because he was *trained* to believe it. He gets used to his confinement. And Sisters, we too allow the black scarf to confine us to a life of oppression because we believe we cannot take it off.

*Please read Isaiah 61:1-4

As I read this beautiful passage, I am convicted to the core. It describes my very heart in this study. Jesus came to preach good news to the poor, to proclaim freedom for captives and to release prisoners from darkness. By His grace we can cast the scarf of black aside. We can rely on His truth to remove the backpack.

*Today, I would like you to revisit the list of bricks from Day One of our homework. For each brick of oppression, I would like you to write a truth from God that smashes that brick to pieces. For example, my biggest struggle with oppression has been debilitating fear. But I know that the perfect love of Jesus casts out fear. I know that fear has to do with punishment, according to 1 John 4:18, and that Jesus Christ took the punishment for me.

See how my brick cannot stand the pressure of absolute truth?

Take the time to examine every brick in your backpack. Shine the light of Scripture into the dark places. And as each one is demolished by the Word, give thanks to the One who has delivered us!

Journal…

✝ Week Six Homework/Day Three

Remembering God...

Yesterday we talked about the baby elephant being trained to stay in his pen by having his ankle tied to a post until he believes he cannot go further than the designated circle.

Another fact about elephants, (and this will be the last I promise!), is that they have a very good memory. The portion of their brain called the hippocampus is very good at remembering...especially memories that hold great emotion.

Elephants are generally passive animals, but if something reminds them of a negative experience, they might become depressed or even aggressive.

The Lord also gave us a remarkable ability to remember. We like to think about special occasions and events and all the good memories.

Unfortunately, we also remember the painful things. And those painful memories can creep up at any time, convincing us to put on the old backpack again.

Sisters, I believe our memories can be the source of re-occurring oppression. So what do we do about it?

"Give thanks to the Lord, call on His name; make known among the nations what He has done. Sing to Him, sing praise to Him; tell of all His wonderful acts. Glory in His holy name; let the hearts of those who seek the Lord rejoice. Look to the Lord and His strength; seek His face

always. Remember the wonders He has done..." *(1Chronicles 16: 8-12)*

Please do not let the past creep back in and burden you again. It is done. Over. And when Jesus said His yoke was easy and His burden was light, he meant it. For now. And forever.

Do you realize this is our very last homework assignment for the Scarves of White study? We still have one more Session together, looking at the Scarf of White, pure and holy. But this is the end of our homework.

*Today I'd like you to look back over all the assignments. Read what you wrote. Perhaps stop and pray over the issues that affected you most. And for your final journal entry, take some time to turn **1 Chronicles 16:8-12** into your personal prayer. Use it as a guideline to truly give thanks from your heart. Speak to God like you've never spoken before. Sing to Him. Rejoice in Him. And remember what He has done for you on this journey.

I have been so blessed to share this with you. I hope and pray with all my heart you are ending this study different than you were before.
I am so excited for our last session. The Scarf of White is my favorite!!! And I know it's yours too. I love the fact that we will end this seven-week study with such grace, brilliance and hope.

See you for Week Seven.

Journal…

∼ Homework Discussion Questions ∼

Week Six: Oppression

(To be shared at the beginning of Week Seven)

1. What names did you give to the bricks of oppression in your backpack? Share if you are willing.
2. What absolute truths did you find to demolish those bricks?
3. Is it tempting to let painful memories pull you back under the cloud of oppression? Using 1 Chronicles 16:8-12 as an example, how can we turn bad memories into moments of thanksgiving?
4. Any other thoughts on the issue of oppression?

Looking Ahead

"...The hour has come for you to wake up from your slumber because our salvation is nearer now than when we first believed. The night is nearly over; the day is almost here. So let us put aside the deeds of darkness, and put on the armor of light...rather, clothe yourselves with the Lord Jesus Christ..." Romans 13:11, 12&14 (NIV)

~Seven~
Scarf of White...*Christ*

Oh the joy that fills my heart today as we end our study together. Yes, I will miss you, but no, I will not miss the issues we have dealt with the last few weeks. Praise the Lord for His mighty power to abolish strongholds!

So where are we at with our colorful scarves? Is our drawer still full of them? Do they still tempt us every day?

Perhaps, but listen. I pray with all my heart that you are more aware of the things that have held you back, and in the Name of Jesus, that these issues will flee!

I hope the next time you *almost* let you anger get the best of you, you will stop. You will remember that love covers over a multitude of things, and anger will not win.

And maybe, before you even go to bed tonight, you will be faced with a wave of discontentment. You will look around and be tempted to say, "Is this all there is?" But! You will stop. You will thank God for the very things that make you so unhappy. And discontentment will not win.

I can almost bet you will be hit with insecurity somewhere down the road. And the same old lies will return, making you think you are not worthy, and you are not capable. Doubt will threaten to overcome you.

But you will stop. You will look to God, the Creator of *who you really are in Christ*. And insecurity will not win.

Pride may tempt you to lift your chin and cast judgment on those around you. It may give you a feeling of entitlement and *almost* cause you to stumble. But you will stop. You will lower your chin. You will bow down…on your knees, on your face before God, Who alone is worthy to be praised. And pride will not win.

Lastly, if oppression raises its ugly head again, and you are burdened with the weight of the world on your shoulders, you will stop. You will remember that only Jesus carried the weight of the entire world on His shoulders. And you will thank Him. You will lean on Him. You will remove the backpack. And oppression will not win.

Ladies, before we each go our separate ways, I want to leave us with a shining example of being clothed in white. Probably my most favorite passage in the Bible, I get goose-bumps every time I read it.

*Please read Revelation 19:11-16

This passage makes me want to sing, "Rider on a white horse, Faithful and True…"

And Sisters, I am no expert in eschatology or the study of end times, but when the Word says the armies of heaven were following Him, riding on white horses and dressed in fine linen white and clean, I so hope it is speaking of us! I want to follow Jesus on a white horse! I am even willing to be the very last one, riding a little pony.

But no matter what, we are His bride. The church is the bride of Jesus, dressed in white, pure and clean.

This sparkly, white scarf is nothing compared to the holiness and newness of life we will receive in eternity.

1 Corinthians 15: 51-58 states, "Listen, I tell you a mystery: We will not all sleep, but we will all be changed- in a flash, in the twinkling of an eye, at the last trumpet. For the trumpet will sound, the dead will be raised imperishable, and we will be changed. For the perishable must clothe itself with imperishable, and the mortal with immortality. When the perishable has been clothed with the imperishable, and the mortal with immortality, then the saying that is written will come true. "Death has been swallowed up in victory. Where O death is your victory? Where O death is your sting? The sting of death is sin, and the power of sin is the law. But thanks be to God! He gives us the victory through our Lord Jesus Christ. Therefore, my dear brothers, (my sisters), stand firm. Let nothing move you. Always give yourselves fully to the work of the Lord, because you know that your labor in the Lord is not in vain."

Let nothing move you.

We have been tossed around by our issues far too long, don't you think?

They have pushed us around, caused us to stumble, hindered our walk with the Lord, and hurt others.

Let nothing move you.

The Story of Stephen, in Acts 6, is such a beautiful example of unwavering faith.

*Please read Acts 6:8-15

Stephen, a man full of God's grace and power, displaying great wonders and miraculous signs, was opposed by many. *But they could not stand up against his wisdom or the Spirit by whom he spoke.*

I want to stop here for a minute Ladies. Our issues, no matter how deep-seeded they are, cannot stand up to the wisdom of God or His Spirit. And the Holy Spirit lives within us.

Sinful anger cannot stand up to the wisdom that says, ***"Your anger does not bring about the righteous life that God desires."***

Discontentment has no strength when wisdom says, ***"God has given us everything we need for life and godliness through our knowledge of Him who called us by His own glory and goodness."***

Wisdom contradicts insecurity by reminding us that, *"**We are God's workmanship, created in Christ Jesus to do good works.**"*

Pride does not stand a chance when the wisdom and authority of God's Word says, ***"I am the Lord Your God. Serve me only!"***

And lastly, the burden of oppression falls away with every word of wisdom spoken against it, saying, ***"Come to Me all you who are weary and burdened and I will give you rest. For My yoke is easy and my burden is light."***

The Jews stirred up lies and falsehood about Stephen so that eventually he was seized and brought before the Sanhedrin. They produced false witnesses saying he had broken the law.

But all who looked at Stephen that day saw that his face was like the face of an angel.

And with the countenance of one in perfect peace, Stephen replied to them in Acts Chapter 7.

"You stiff-necked people, with uncircumcised hearts and ears! You are just like your fathers: You always resist the Holy Spirit! Was there ever a prophet your fathers did not persecute? They even killed those who predicted the coming of the Righteous One. And now you have betrayed and murdered Him. You who have received the law that was given through angels but have not obeyed it." When the members of the Sanhedrin heard this, they were furious and gnashed their teeth at him. But Stephen, full of the Holy Spirit, looked up to heaven and saw the glory of God, and Jesus standing at the right hand of God. At this they covered their ears and, yelling at the top of their voices, they all rushed at him, dragged him out of the city and began to stone him. Meanwhile, the witnesses laid their clothes at the feet of a young man named Saul. While they were stoning him, Stephen prayed, "Lord Jesus, receive my spirit." They he fell on his knees and cried out, "Lord, do not hold this sin against them." When he had said this, he fell asleep. (Acts 7:51-60)

Ladies, I don't know about you, but I want to be like Stephen in my faith. I do not want to be like those who were stiff-necked, resisting the Holy Spirit.

And when the stones of anger, discontentment, insecurity, pride, and oppression come, I want to be steadfast like Stephen, who was full of the Holy Spirit, looking up to heaven and seeing the glory of God, even while being stoned to death.
Sisters, at the mention of Jesus' name, at the Word of His mouth, and in the power of Almighty God, I pray for freedom from everything that holds us back from serving the Living God.

I pray that our faces will be like that of angels. Full of peace, looking up toward heaven, and covered in light.

Let nothing move you.

And tomorrow, as you open your drawer I pray with all my heart you will find it empty. Completely empty. Because the only scarf you need is already covering you…the Scarf of White, Jesus Christ.

∽ Tips and Ideas for Small Group Leaders ∽

1. Consider purchasing colorful scarves to be used as visuals during your class sessions.

2. If you are really creative, you can decorate in the theme color each week. Table runners, and simple centerpieces might add to the room. Example: For the Session on Anger, a red runner can be placed on the table, along with mini boxes of red-hots or Hot Tamales.

3. Have a white board available for the Scriptures highlighted each week.

4. Designate your co-leader to send out prayer requests via e-mail. Emphasize confidentiality among the group.

5. Be prepared for a non-believer or brand new believer to join your study. Have a new believer's packet ready, along with an extra Bible. Be willing to meet with them outside of class, and be prepared to share the Gospel.

6. When in doubt about something, always look to your Women's Ministry leaders to help you out. It's ok to say that you don't know the answer, but will get back to them.

7. Cover everything in prayer. Every participant, every session and every conversation.

8. Start your class time with a couple of simple worship songs. Use a CD if you aren't musical.

About the Author

Jennifer considers herself a Kansas girl, married to a Colorado hunk, and Mama to four. Extra blessed with two darling grand babies, her cup runs over! Jennifer adores her Savior and desires to be exactly who she was created to be. As a writer, speaker and musician, she is devoted to bringing messages of encouragement to women everywhere.

Look for more of Jennifer's books, available soon!

If you would like more information, or to schedule an encouragement event for your Women's Ministry, contact Jennifer here:

www.jenniferwaddleonline.com

encouragementmama@gmail.com

30380525R00081

Made in the USA
Lexington, KY
09 February 2019